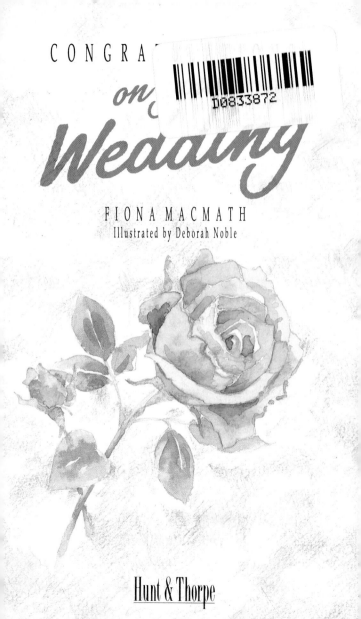

CONGRA...
on
Wedding

FIONA MACMATH
Illustrated by Deborah Noble

Hunt & Thorpe

1 Corinthians ch. 13 v 4, 5, 6 & 7

Love is patient and kind; love is not
jealous or boastful; it is not
arrogant or rude. Love does not
insist on its own way; it is
not irritable or resentful; it
does not rejoice at wrong, but
rejoices in the right. Love
bears all things, believes all
things, hopes all things,
endures all things.

Helen & Thomas

May today be the start
of a wonderful journey
together.

May God Bless you
and your marriage.

with very best wishes.
John & Jenny (Hurley)
(Friends of Mays)

The Point

'It's very soon done, sir, isn't it?' inquired Mr
Folair of Mr Lillyvick, leaning over the table to
address him.
'What is soon done, sir?' returned Mr Lillyvick.
'The tying up, the fixing oneself with a wife.'
replied Mr Folair. 'It don't take long, does it?'

NICHOLAS NICKELBY (CHAPTER 25) BY CHARLES DICKENS

Your wedding day is probably one of the
shortest days of your life. Here you are, doing
the most momentous thing you have ever done,
and it all seems to flash past you. And the
wedding ceremony seems the shortest bit of all.

Months of preparation and a great deal of
money might have gone into this day, so
perhaps it isn't worth it? Why not slide into a
life together and put the money toward a house
instead? But how dull and calculating! And
how this misses the point.

The Promise

A wedding is two things: a celebration and a promise. You have found somebody to love and that someone loves you back. Can anything be more joyous? And you love each other so much that you are willing to throw away the neat, separate worlds you have built for yourselves and jumble your lives together. Such love somehow generates more love, and you invite your friends and family to share it and celebrate it.

This, at least, is how it feels most of the time. But you can't see your partner's love for you; you can't shut it safely in a box. Chances are you may have found yourself wondering, 'does he/she really love me?' (It's worth remembering that your partner has the same thoughts!).

This is where the promise comes in. At the heart of a marriage are still the marriage vows. The recollection and living out of that promise – 'to have and to hold' – will provide a rock in years to come.

For the doubts never quite go away, because we live in a world of uncertainties. But the remembrance of that promise on that particular day will transform the doubts from being a profound, threatening insecurity into an intermittent, nagging reminder: 'You do love me, don't you sweetheart? Because I love you.'

Cana

The joy of marriage and its underlying seriousness were both stressed by Jesus. When the wine ran out at the wedding feast in Cana, he didn't declare, "Oh, well, that will save you a bit of money to put down on your new house":

"Nearby stood six stone water jars, the kind used by the Jews for ceremonial washing, each holding from twenty to thirty gallons (75 to 115 litres).

Jesus said to the servants, 'Fill the jars with water'; so they filled them to the brim.

Then he told them, 'Now draw some out and take it to the master of the banquet.'

"They did so, and the master of the banquet tasted the water that had been turned into wine. He did not realize where it had come from, though the servants who had drawn the water knew. Then he called the bridegroom aside and said, 'Everyone brings out the choice wine first and then the cheaper wine after the guests have had too much to drink; but you have saved the best till now.'"

JOHN 2:6–10

8

A New Start

Jesus might seem to be using his miraculous powers here in a frivolous way. But marriage to him was important and his teaching on it was radical and idealistic – and so difficult that his followers exclaimed: "If this is the situation between a husband and wife, it is better not to marry!" Matthew 19:10

Jesus went back to the original plan at creation, expressed in the story of Adam and Eve: we are made in God's image and the marriage of a man and a woman is a picture of the wholeness of God, the re-uniting of the male and female characters which God possesses.

Two into One

'Haven't you read,' he replied, 'that at the beginning
the Creator "made them male and female", and said,
"for this reason a man will leave his father and
mother and be united to his wife, and the two will
become one flesh"? So they are no longer two, but
one. Therefore what God has joined together, let man
not separate.'

MATTHEW 19:4–6

As such, taught Jesus, a marriage union should
never be broken or corrupted. How can it be
compatible with love to break the promises of
life–long commitment?

Freedom to Be

Jesus might have said that the two shall become three, or four, or more. Although marriage ties two people together, it also frees them to be more open in their love and concern for others. As your marriage progresses, you will find that you are less anxious and more effective in your love and support for the people around you.

This is the strange truth the ancient Israelites knew so well: to be bonded to someone brings freedom. In this case it is freedom from uncertainty, freedom from the fear of rejection, freedom from the predatory mating game that so often displaces old-fashioned courtship – all things that can inhibit our love for others. When a steady and increasing source of love is found and applied, our personalities open like flowers, and facets of character, long-hidden, begin to emerge.

Giving is Receiving

As you and your partner give yourselves to each other on your wedding day and as you continue to practice self-sacrifice throughout your marriage, you really will find that you get back more than you give. If anything is the clue to many of the things in a successful marriage, not least sexual enjoyment and the welcoming of children, then it is this.

Love is patient, love is kind. It does not envy, it does not boast, it is not proud. It is not rude, it is not self-seeking, it is not easily angered, it keeps no record of wrongs. Love does not delight in evil but rejoices with the truth. It always protects, always trusts, always hopes, always perseveres. Love never fails.

1 CORINTHIANS 13:4–8

Making the Pieces Fit

Love never fails. But what about the jumble of insecurity and dependency that people mistake for love? One third of all marriages in Britain end in divorce. How can you know that yours is not going to be one of the unsuccessful ones?

There are all sorts of reasons why marriages fail (and an unhappy marriage that staggers on is just as much a failure as a marriage that breaks up). But at the heart of many of them is the switch from giving to taking, from self-sacrifice to selfishness. And at the heart of *this* is often fear.

Human beings are more complicated than pieces of a jigsaw. They don't always fit neatly together. When two people fit together both have to work at it. The bumps come when discussing the range of problems life throws at us: Who does what round the house? Who handles the money? What happens to individual interests? Should you have children? When? Before the wedding is the time to talk about these things. It is not good to allow the preparations for the wedding day to squeeze out the less exciting preparations for married life.

Together

Always remember, though, that it is not God's way to set impossibly high standards and watch while we fail to reach them. God gives us spiritual gifts to help us. The most obvious of these is love. But it has to be admitted that forgiveness is another crucial one.

Together, these two create trust. And it is in an atmosphere of trust that problems get turned into challenges – to be met by both of you together. That is, after all, what makes married life interesting.

Back to the Beginning

By now, you will probably be bewildered by the huge amount of advice you receive on how to organise your wedding. But just one more piece to add to the heap: this is the start of your life together, so try and spend *some* of the wedding celebration in each other's company!

"Near and far, near and far,
I am happy where you are;
Likewise, I have never larnt
How to be it where you aren't.

Yes, and I'm afraid I pout
When I'm indoors and you are out;
But how contentedly I view
Any room containing you.
Let none, not even you, disparage
Such valid reason for a marriage."

From Tin Wedding Whistle by Ogden Nash

Copyright © 1991 Hunt & Thorpe
Text © Fiona and Paul Handley
Illustrations © Deborah Noble 1991
First published by Hunt & Thorpe 1991
ISBN 1 85608 076 5

The CIP catalogue record for this book is
available from the British Library.

Manufactured in Italy.